Dear Christine,

Keep up the Good

Reiki Blessings

Steven

Hare Lip to Healer

Hare Lip to Healer

STEVEN RUDELHOFF

StoryTerrace

Text Nadia Salehian, on behalf of StoryTerrace

Design StoryTerrace

Copyright © Steven Rudelhoff and StoryTerrace

Text is private and confidential

First print November 2022

StoryTerrace

www.StoryTerrace.com

CONTENTS

PART ONE

'*Some changes look negative on the surface but you will soon realise that space is being created in your life for something new to emerge.*'

– Eckhart Tolle

1

SCHOOL

My journey into this life was not a straightforward one. I was born on 8th February 1957 in the Jewish Hospital in Stoke Newington in London at midday. I was born with a hare lip and a cleft palate, but I was lucky that I had the love and attention of my mum, who was only 17 at the time, and my grandmother, as I needed a lot of medical care and operations from the very start of my life.

As an infant, I had to have operations every six months. Due to my growing bones, the doctors had to continually try to repair and adjust the roof of my mouth because of the hole in it, which I've still got. The right side of my nostril is completely closed and could never be repaired. As well as the ongoing operations, I also had to have frequent speech therapy.

I had a brilliant surgeon called Dr Battle, and the operations were so invasive that it really was like going into battle when he was operating on me. With so many hare lip reconstructions, the results would be clearly visible and the patient would have a straight line scar and their top lip would be really tucked in. I was very fortunate because, with Dr Battle as my surgeon, I was one of the first children in this country to have my lip fixed into the shape of a W. As a result, it is barely noticeable.

Eventually, my operations became annual until I was 15 years old. For my last operation, my nose was completely broken and reset, and I was unconscious for three days. When my mum came to see me, she nearly passed out because of how severe my face looked. I was swollen, bruised and totally unrecognisable.

I then needed plastic surgery to correct the end of my nose. One thing that proved to be impossible was fixing my right nostril. Each time the surgeon would open it up, it kept collapsing in on itself, which is why I have never been able to breathe through it. I have had to breathe through my mouth my whole life, which has been very difficult.

We lived in Walthamstow, but the hospital I used to go to was in Surrey, so my parents couldn't come with me because it was too far and I had two younger siblings that needed to be taken care of. I would be taken to the pickup point and driven to the hospital by ambulance. I would be there for a week to have an operation. I would see other children's parents coming to visit, which made me feel very lonely.

Alongside having these operations, I had to go to a dentist in Grays Inn Road in London at Eastman's dental hospital. I would go every month and would be in a big hall with about

30 dentists and patients having their treatments carried out at the same time. It was frightening because I could hear all the old-fashioned belt-driven drills, and people would be screaming out and yelling in pain.

My dentist was Miss Mills. I was under her supervision from the age of eight until 12 years old and sometimes, I would be in the chair for two hours. On one occasion, I had cemented metal clips put on every tooth, top and bottom, with a brace before all my teeth were turned at once. The pain was absolutely horrendous. As a result, I've been traumatised by dentists.

Because of all the time spent at the dentists and having operations, I missed out on most of my schooling. I was always in the bottom class. I couldn't spell, write or read properly and was constantly picked on because of the way I looked and talked. I completed my school work experience in a hospital in the physiotherapy unit, which I really enjoyed, and when I went back to school, I told my teachers that I wanted to train to be a physiotherapist, but they told me that I wasn't intelligent enough, so I was knocked down once again.

The only thing that I was really good at was sport, and I made it into the school's football team every year. I also played for the county. I have played at West Ham and just down the road from Wembley. I had trials for Chelsea and Watford as a teenager, so I had the talent for football; plus it had the extra benefit of being an outlet for me. As well as football, I was taking part in swimming, gymnastics and general athletics. Whatever sport I tried, I excelled at it. RE and sports were the only subjects on my school report I got an A in.

I remember walking into my junior school when I was about seven, just after lunch, and there were 10 kids on one side and 10 on the other side. It was like a human walkway, built of people calling me names and abusing me.

I was not religious, as both my parents were atheists, so I don't know why I said these words, because no one had ever taught them to me, but as I was walking through that corridor of abuse I said to myself, 'Forgive them Lord for they know not what they do'. It wasn't until later in life that I found that it was Jesus that had said it.

When I was about four, I could often be found sitting on my little three-wheeler trike in the prayer position for hours at a time. Just praying. I don't know what I was praying for or saying, but when I look back and think of all the experiences I've had as an adult, I know I had come from Spirit. As a young boy, I was still connected to that world, so I was just giving gratitude and praying. As I had never been exposed to religion, my parents and neighbours would watch me with confusion.

I had some really awful teachers in school. My woodwork teacher would pull continuously on our sideburns if we got into trouble and in another class, the teacher would make me stand on a chair with my arms held out in front of me to put a brick in each hand.

I was in a rough group for my metalwork class. We would have rods of metal in the forge that would be white-hot and one of the boys would ask me to hold the rod, but I wouldn't know it was hot. I even had cigarettes put out on me. I couldn't report the abuse because it was considered normal and the teachers were no better than the students. It was just how things were. Because I had missed so much school, I wasn't stupid, but I hadn't had the time to learn, so I was in the classes with all the roughest children. But, in a way, that's what made me strong.

I didn't have a place where I felt safe and happy. My parents knew what was happening, but my dad was very physical and violent, so he condoned the bullying. Sometimes I would ask my mum if I could miss school and she would let me, but we had to keep it a secret from my dad.

I used to have a paper round and a milk round before school. One of my mates had a bike that I wanted, and he was selling it for two bob. So I drew that out of my savings and bought his bike. Mum was wary because I hadn't asked my dad first, but because it was money I had earned and saved, I didn't think I needed his permission. When my dad got home, he was so angry with me that he belted and whipped me all around the room. I then had to return the bike and ask for my money back.

I was very close to my mum. She just wanted a quiet life. She has been on healing courses with me. She died last year in 2021, and I was with her, helping her cross over, which was really special. My mum has come through to me a few times in messages and she's happy, but she's sorry that she wasn't strong enough to protect me. But she was young when she had me, and she didn't know any better.

Although my childhood was difficult and my father was stern, he was also a very typical dad of the time. What comes across now as being overly harsh was considered normal then. He always provided for us, and he was committed to us all, and I am grateful for the career I have had, which was a result of his efforts.

There were many happy holidays and Christmases together, and I am living proof that the next generation can evolve and change how we love our families.

My first School at four and half years of age, at Markhouse Road, Walthamstow, London

2

BAD SPIRITS

I was introduced to the spirit world from a very young age. My father and his friends introduced my mum to the Ouija board and they would use it at home, which brought bad spirits into the house. We witnessed strange things, like pots of sugar flying across the room, doors opening and shutting. Even our poodle Toby would not go upstairs.

When any of us children wanted to go to the toilet, we would have to go together because as soon as you went up the stairs, your body went cold. It was frightening being in the house, looking after my brother and sister with all of that dark spirit around us. Even though I was still very young, my parents saw no issue with leaving me to mind my two younger siblings while they were out on Saturday nights. The three of us would stay very close to each other for fear of anything happening.

It was a usual habit for my parents to have four or five friends at the house, drink a bottle of whiskey, watch cheap porno-type films that were made back in those days and then get out the Ouija board. After two or three months of this going on, three of my dad's friends committed suicide by hanging. Because of the Ouija board, he was surrounded by a negative energy field, and a spirit kept coming through to my mum, warning her that my dad was evil and that she needed to get away from him, but she never left him. After the death of his friends, my dad stopped doing it. He was so controlling and frightening that my mother wouldn't have been able to stop him from using it had these awful deaths not occurred.

My dad and mum, brother and sister. Left to right are me, Ian, Sue, Mum and Dad.

3

ADULTING AT 14

I believe that I didn't make it through my football trials for Chelsea and Watford because my dad refused to support me. I went to the football trials, but I had no confidence and felt that even trying was pointless because I felt so defeated by his overbearing and aggressive manner. He had been a butcher all his life, and I think he was jealous of the idea that I could be something more than he was, so when I was 14, he told me that he had got me a job as a butcher and that was what I was going to do.

In those days, children would finish school at the age of 14 with the option to carry on or leave. I had failed my 11-plus exams, so when it came to making the choice to stay on or not, my dad told me he had already found me a job and that was that. I was already working every Saturday in my dad's butcher shop from the age of eight. I would have to stand on a box to be able to reach the table, and I would be boning out legs of beef.

I would have to get up at five in the morning, leave at six

and get home at seven at night. I would do all the cleaning, organise the fridges and make the burgers. By nine or 10, I would get paid £1 a week. It was very hard work, but I could never go against my dad's demands, and later in life I discovered in my soul plan that this would be one of my challenges. My brother ended up working with my dad, but my sister is a lot more like my dad and ironically, she wouldn't stand for any of that, so she left home as soon as she could.

I traded in one hardship for another. Growing up, I had so much passion in me, but no matter how hard I tried, it seemed that everything I did kept getting either blocked or simply wouldn't happen. I had all this fire that was being extinguished in me. I really believed that there was nothing I couldn't achieve if I was just given the opportunity. But with so much resistance, I thought, there's no point in me trying to do anything because whatever I tried to do wasn't going to happen.

From when I was 14 and working full-time, I had to ride my bike 14 miles to and from work, on top of doing a full day of physical labour, all for £7.50 a week. One night, I was so tired while cycling down a dark road that I fell asleep and ended up in a bush! I was working with a nice man called John Shepherdton who would sometimes drive me home. By that time, my dad had been made a district manager and was in charge of about 20 shops.

I also had to serve customers and in those days, I could

have a customer with 10 items and I just had to add it all up in my head. There was no option of a till to work the amount or how much change to give back, so I learned how to do all of that myself. While I was serving customers, I was able to add up 10, 20 items in my head, and although I could hardly read or write, I was able to spell anything to do with butchery.Over the course of time, it really helped to boost my confidence.

Contrary to my initial belief, I did enjoy being a butcher, and I set myself a challenge to get to a higher position than my dad by doing things differently. He was as aggressive at work as he was at home. He was very good at what he did and got good results from his managers, but he used fear as a motivator. I made it my mission to change that attitude with my staff and colleagues.

My butchery training was in South Oxhey in an old-fashioned butchers', and my manager was very harsh. He would be standing at the back of the shop in the corridor, watching me work while he smoked all day. He would have a bottle of brandy and milk a day, go to the pub and then come back for the end of the day.

Despite his heavy drinking, he had a sharp eye, and if I did anything wrong, he would spot it. When I would tie up a roll of beef, I would have to take it to him to check it, and if he could get his finger under any one of the strings, he would get a knife and cut it and would swear at me and tell me to do it again and to make sure it was right that time.

If I didn't get it right, I would be punished with extra cleaning. For example, when I was cleaning the wooden blocks, he would get me to clean the legs of the blocks with a toothbrush. He used to have me in tears, and his wife, who worked in the butchers' as well, would always calm me down and tell me he didn't mean it. I really appreciated her kindness. My work environment was mirroring my home life.

Even though he was really tough on me, it was with him that I really learned my craft. From there, I became a manager of a shop in Borehamwood when I was around 16. I even had the flat above the shop. I then went on to run a shop in Watford and made a success of that too. Then, when I had a shop on Ealing Broadway, we were taking £10,000 a week, and this was the '80s. So in today's terms, that would be about £40,000, so it was very busy. My dad got to become sales district manager, running 20 shops, but I've achieved all of that and more.

Me and my dear mum.

4

CARLA

Carla's mum used to shop in my butchers', so we were well acquainted. What I didn't know at that time was that Carla worked two doors down from me in a hairdressers' and that she was hanging around with a lot of people on drugs. Her mother wanted to draw her away from that crowd and would always say to me that I should meet her daughter. I wasn't really interested and I don't know how it came about, but one day I said, 'Yeah, all right. I'll take her out.'

I didn't expect to fall in love and get married. Carla was my first real relationship, and I felt secure and happy with her. I experienced a kind of tenderness and affection that had never been given to me, and we had some really great moments together.

We lived in the flat above my butchers' in Borehamwood with our sons, David and Daniel, and for a while we were very happy. We wanted to have our kids young so that we could still be young parents while they were growing up.

We couldn't afford to buy a house there, so we moved to Ely with Carla's mother in her big six-bedroom house. I was able to get a mortgage for half the house, and Carla's mum paid for the other half.

The honeymoon period ended abruptly once we moved. There was so much wrong with the house, which we didn't know about, but my father had pointed out these issues to Carla's mum. Unfortunately, she she didn't believe him, which not only caused arguments between them but then also resulted in having builders there for over a year while we were living there with two little kids of three and four.

Because I didn't have a car, I would have to walk about a mile or so down the road to the train station, get the six o'clock train to Cambridge, then walk another mile up to where I was working and do a day's work and come home. Her mum took the surveyors to court over all the troubles with the house, and that became a two- to three-year court battle.

While I was at work, her mum's anger and frustrations were coming out on Carla. Carla started working a night job at Tesco, and I was working all day. I would come home, put the kids to bed and tidy the house, and Carla would be coming in as I was going to work. It was having a negative impact on our marriage. I spoke with Carla and said, 'this can't go on.' No matter how poor we were, we couldn't carry on like that because we were drifting apart. I remember coming home with flowers for Carla and asking her to give up her job, that we would make it work somehow, but she didn't want to do that.

The following day, I came home from work and Carla and the kids were gone. She had left me and moved into a council refuge home. I couldn't even see my kids. It turned out that she met someone on the night shift at Tesco. So I was left without my wife and children, but I was still living with my mother-in-law, who lived on one side of the house while I kept to the other side.

I used to come in from work, make dinner and tell myself I was fine, that I wasn't cracking up, but when I got into bed, I must have cried every night for at least eight weeks. I loved her very much, so I was totally devastated. I vowed that another female would never break me again.

Carla was rehomed eventually and was given a council house. We got divorced and came to the agreement that I would have the kids every other weekend.

When I was in my 30s, I met a girl called Rachel, who was 15 years younger than me. She was besotted with me, and I was worried that her mum and dad would be really unhappy, but they were lovely to me. I signed the house over to Carla's mum and moved out with nothing except my personal belongings. I was put up in Rachel's parents' house. Within a couple of years, Rachel and I were able to buy a house in the town of March, which was a starter home. While we were living with Rachel's parents, I was still seeing my kids every other weekend.

Rachel's dad was a fishmonger and owned a rascal van, so he would put blankets in the back for Rachel, and I to take the kids to the beach. I couldn't afford to take them to a funfair, so we would just spend the day on the open beach. I started telling them from an early age what had happened with Carla. I wanted them to know I didn't leave them.

I left Dewhurst when I met Rachel and started working for the Cambridge Co-op in the supermarket. I managed to turn their sales around from £400 to £5,000 a week within a couple of years. I eventually got promoted to Regional Fresh Food Controller, and I was managing 90 supermarkets and about 5,000 staff.

I had achieved my goal of getting to a higher position than my dad, while doing it in a nice and gentle way. I found that by being understanding and listening to my staff, being on hand to help them when they needed it, they were more willing to do a better job. I was in that job for a year, and things were going really well. I had a company car, an expense account. I really felt like I was on the up. And then the universe stepped in again.

I remember that day as if it was yesterday. I was driving when my beeper started buzzing and I had a message to go into the office straight away. My first thought was that I was being made redundant, and when I got to the office, it turned out I was right. The company was very good to me. They told me it was another round of management restructuring and that my redundancy wouldn't take effect for another month but that I could go home immediately, not to worry about work and to do whatever sorting out I needed to do. So I had a month off with full pay while I tried to find something, but I couldn't find any jobs like that one, and I was out of work for a year.

My relationship with Rachel had come to an inevitable end some time before my redundancy. It was an amicable break-up. She was a lovely girl, but the age gap was starting to show, and she had different things she wanted to do with her life. It was time for me to go into the next phase of my own.

5

SANDRA

Sandra was an employee in one of our Cambridge supermarkets while I was working as the Regional Fresh Food Controller. Part of my role was to frequently visit the stores under my management. Whenever I used to go to the supermarket she worked in, the staff would playfully joke that Sandra liked me. I would dismiss it as work banter and had no intention of getting involved with a member of my staff, so I just let them have their harmless fun.

This went on for about six months until it got to a point where all I'd hear during my visits was how she would not stop talking about me. Eventually, I was convinced to ask her out. My original intention was just to go as a one-off gesture, but the date did not go as expected. Firstly, considering how eager she was to go out with me, she was very quiet and quite frankly, rather dull! We met at a pub, and I ended up doing all the talking and getting nothing back from her. She was totally closed off and in all honesty, all I could think about was how long I'd have to wait before politely ending the evening and going home.

Secondly, as I drove her home, I kept hoping that she would tell her colleagues that it was a disaster and that would be the end of her ongoing crush. But as I was saying goodnight to Sandra, for some reason I had an impulse to lean in and kiss her. It took us both by surprise, and even while we were kissing, I wondered what had even possessed me to go through with it at all. Following our spontaneous kiss, we then proceeded to go out a few more times. As we spent more time together, she explained that she had been hurt by another man and was having a very difficult time getting over the break-up; that was why she was so reserved with me.

The universe clearly had other plans for us because we ended up in a marriage that spanned 15 years! I believe the joint purpose of us being brought together was for her to open up to love again and for me to accept help and learn how to be vulnerable and feel nurtured. Sandra was brought to me at a time when I was going to need someone like her in my life more than I could have imagined.

Our first test during the early years of our marriage was when I was made redundant and out of work for a year. I was unable to find another job and had no idea what I was going to do. Then I saw a job advertised in the paper for a butchery manager in Wales, which came with a three-bedroom flat as accommodation. Sandra wasn't happy with what she was doing at the time, so we saw it as an opportunity to try something different. We travelled to Wales for my interview and spent a weekend in the beautiful village of Llanidloes, with cobblestone streets and a lovely, traditional feel.

I was offered the job, and we were excited for the change. We thought we would be there for a few months, but it ended up being 10 years. I was really busy and very successful at growing the business, so everything was going really well for me. But things took an unfortunate turn. I became unusually exhausted and started experiencing severe pain in my neck, pins and needles, and a loss of power in my hands and arms. Aside from this, I had undergone two knee operations as a result of previous football injuries, so I was already not doing so well physically, but these new symptoms were totally different from anything I had experienced before. I had X-rays taken, and I was diagnosed with a condition called cervical spondylosis, which meant that the vertebrae in my neck were deteriorating.

Years of lifting up to 220-pound carcasses of meat over my shoulders and working in cold temperatures really had a negative effect on my body. I also complicated my situation while playing football. We used to use the old style of leather balls, and when they got wet in the rain, it was like headbutting a heavy weight. The consultant said I could have an operation wherein the surgeon would cut a hole in my throat and thread down a metal rod into my vertebrae to fuse them all together. But there would be an 80% chance of being totally paralysed, and I couldn't take that risk, so I was left with medication for the pain and no solution to my failing health.

I couldn't continue with my job, so my time in Wales had to come to an end. In time, we moved back to our one-bedroom starter home in England. I was experiencing deep depression and even reached a point where I felt suicidal. I had overcome a lot of struggles in my life and I was used to being very active, so losing my ability to work and becoming dependent on someone else due to my pain and lack of mobility was crushing me. With no cure in sight, I had no fight left in me and was ready to give up.

About four weeks after moving back from Wales, I was reading the local paper while Sandra was at work. I kept getting this thought that I needed to go and see a medium. With this recurring voice in my head, I decided to act upon it and thought, at the very least, it would be a morning out of the house to distract me from my dark thoughts. I made an appointment, and my sceptical mind thought, *she only knows me as Steven. I've been in Wales for 10 years and only back home a few weeks, so she wouldn't be able to find out much about me if she tried to do any background search.*

I arrived at the appointment with my crutches and neck brace, and she told me that she wouldn't say anything negative, that any messages she gave me would come from love and light and that she would be speaking through her spiritual guide. I didn't know what to think about all of that and I had no idea what she was talking about, so I just listened.

She began by saying, 'I've got this big tall man in front of me. Very tall. His name's Jack, and he's got greasy hands.'

My granddad, my dad's dad, was called Jack. He was a butcher and very tall. I didn't tell her anything about who he was.

I just sat in silence, and so she continued, 'He's got a pint of beer right in front of him now and is saying happy birthday for Friday.'

My birthday was indeed on that coming Friday.

She went on to say, 'Steven, you're a bit of an oddball, and I am saying that with love, but you feel like you come from another planet and not from this earth.'

I had always felt like I didn't come from here, that I was from somewhere else. This was a feeling I had never shared with others.

She then said, 'You will be travelling all over the world, healing and doing what I'm doing.'

I didn't believe her at the time, as I couldn't imagine doing anything so dramatically different with my life, but even so, when I left her, I felt empowered by the experience. This ignited a change within me.

When I got home, I started thinking of how I could heal myself. I felt inspired to not be a victim of my health condition and to be proactive in finding a way out of my physical confinement. I started looking into different types of self-healing, and that's when I discovered reiki.

I was in my 40s, and I knew my career as a butcher was over, so I had to retrain in something else. I began by enrolling in reiki courses. I could still hardly read or write, but I managed to complete the reiki training through strong-willed determination and a lot of effort. I was committed to waking up early every morning to meditate and practise self-healing. It gave me a reason to get out of bed every day. In turn, there was a shift in my mental health. Unbelievably, I came off all my medication six months later and my energy had come back. I was no longer exhausted by basic things like simply walking down the stairs.

The incredible transformation inspired me to want to learn more. As I began to heal, I started going to the local library to learn basic computer skills. I then did a reflexology course, which was a real challenge, as the courses were of a very high level and there was a lot I had to learn, such as anatomy and physiology. I would stay up all night to complete my homework because my typing was so slow, but I wanted to use the computer rather than write everything so that I could use spell check.

The duration of my illness was a terrible time for Sandra. Before I understood about self-healing, it was difficult for me to accept being in a vulnerable situation, which put a strain on us. It was made even harder by the fact that she had to look after me and I was unable to do anything for myself.

She had an awful job in a paint-spraying factory, and they didn't have proper protective clothing, so I used to see her walking down our street at the end of her shift wearing a big long coat with paint all over her. She was exhausted and most likely overwhelmed by the sudden turn around in her life, working a job she hated and then having to come home and take care of her husband, who had become almost completely immobilised.

It was completely different from the idyllic life we had created in that picture-perfect village in Wales, and it started to affect our relationship. As I was getting more into self-healing and meditation, I started to feel more connected to the energy around me. It was hard for Sandra to understand. She wanted to believe what I was experiencing, but she wasn't ready to open herself up, whereas I was really starting to feel empowered by it all.

During my recovery, while I was still unable to leave the house, Sandra started working at a chicken factory in Wisbech. Due to the shifts she was working, we would often miss each other during the days and evenings, so eventually we started drifting apart. I was hopeful that with the positive transformation I was undergoing, we would be able to find the joy in our relationship again and to mend our marriage.

However, during this time, she had met someone at work and started a relationship with him instead. I didn't realise what was happening until after we had broken up, but she would often come home and talk to me about Gary at work, who was her line manager. I would ask after him as well, not thinking anything of it.

But that is not how we broke up.

Me and Sandra on a walk when we were living in Wales.

6

INGRID

I became interested in learning about trance healing, so I enrolled at the Arthur Findlay College in Stansted. Trance healing is when you are able to get your brain into an alpha state and a spirit can come into your energy field and take over your body to talk through you.

I met a lady at the college from Belgium called Isabel who was a medium. A few months later, we were both at the college again on another course and she had brought her friend Ingrid with her from Belgium.

As soon as Isabel introduced her to me, Ingrid ran off to the toilet. When Isabel asked her what was the matter, Ingrid told her that she had an overwhelming feeling that something was going to happen between her and me. Considering she was married with children and knew nothing about me, the feelings she experienced startled her.

During the course, Ingrid and I were in separate groups. She connected with her spirit guide, Saint Germain, and asked him if she knew me from a previous life. The message she received back was that we had a past life together as a Native American couple. I was the woman, and she was the man, and Ingrid had been killed by an axe blow to the head. She was suffering from a headache all day, which she attributed to the trauma coming through her.

During one of our breaks, we stood under a big oak tree, instinctively choosing to hold hands, and Ingrid told me all that had come through to her from her spirit guide. It was a lot for me to take in and, at the time, I really wasn't sure how I felt. I was still at the start of my healing and spiritual journey, and it was a lot to accept from a total stranger. At the end of the course, which was only a few days long, we kissed before she went back to her husband in Belgium and I went home to Sandra. But over the next few days, I felt like a teenager falling in love for the first time. I felt like I was climbing the walls!

I called Isabel in Belgium, and I told her how I was feeling and that I wanted to speak with Ingrid. It turned out that Ingrid was feeling the same way. We were able to speak to each other over the phone quite frequently and with ease because it turned out that both Sandra and Ingrid's husband worked night shifts.

Ingrid thought that there might be a ritual to cut off that past life. Because the previous relationship had ended so suddenly by death, perhaps we were brought together in this life to help with the spiritual passing of their relationship. It made sense to me, and I just assumed whatever I was feeling for Ingrid was connected to that previous life and the love we had for each other then. I rationalised it as such and did not think that it was going to impact our respective marriages.

I decided to go to Belgium in February, and I told Sandra that Isabel had asked me to go and teach a reiki course. There was no way I could explain the truth without worrying Sandra. Perhaps in that instance, had I been honest, I would have understood that her intuition was telling of things to come, which I could not foresee.

When I arrived in Belgium, Isabel lent us the use of her apartment for the afternoon to do some sort of ritual. We were totally unsure about what was going to happen or how intimate we would be. We ended up having a bath together. I can't explain why we decided to do that other than it was instinctive and felt like the most natural thing to do at the time. Nothing happened sexually, but there was a magnetic pull that was too strong for us to ignore going forward; it was more than having to heal a past trauma now. We both went our separate ways and continued to talk over the phone. By then, Sandra was starting to get suspicious that perhaps something was going on behind her back.

Then came the call that was going to change the lives of everyone involved. Ingrid told me she had told her husband and children about me and was moving to England on 1st April. It all happened very suddenly, so it was difficult for her husband to understand her reasons, but it was made even harder by the simple fact that Ingrid is a bit of a dreamer. She thought everything would run smoothly, which of course it didn't.

I went to Belgium a couple of times and met her husband, which was incredibly difficult, as he couldn't make sense of what was happening. He was hurt and angry, which made me hesitant and question whether we were doing the right thing. I worried that perhaps the universal messages we received were wrong. But as hard as it was, Ingrid stuck to her beliefs and was in the UK on 1st April.

When I told Sandra that I was moving out, she sobbed, seemingly heartbroken. I spent nights on the sofa hearing her cry upstairs, which made me feel terrible. Again, I worried that maybe I was not doing the right thing. What I did not know was that Sandra was already in a relationship with Gary, and only a week after I left, he moved into the house I bought with her. I signed over the house to Sandra, making it the second time I had left a relationship with nothing.

Me and Ingrid on our wedding day in Kenya 14/02/2005

Ingrid in our Healing room in Cemetery Lodge during our early days of healing.

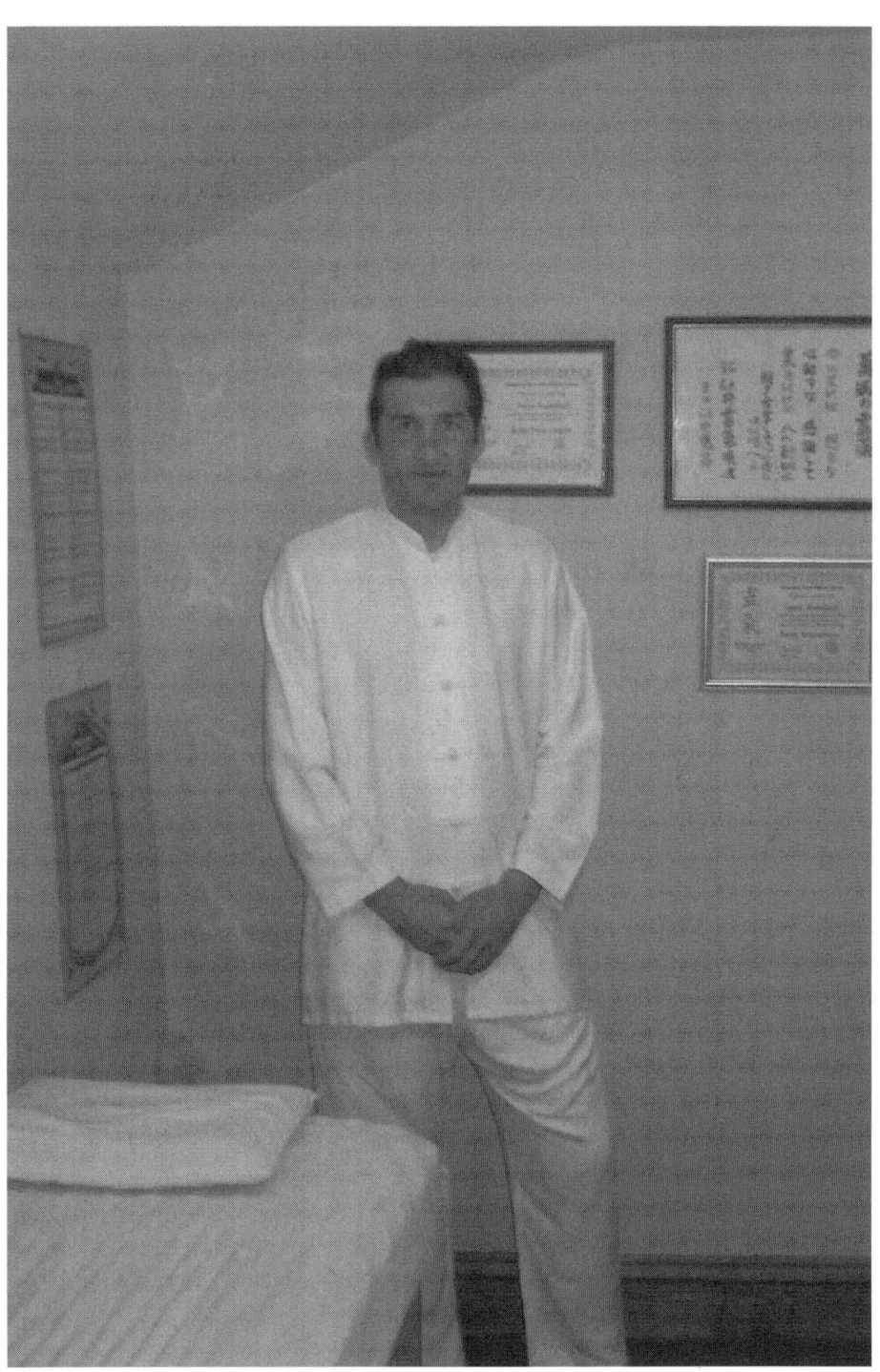

In my Healing room in 2005 in my early days and with hair.

Me and Ingrid so happy at my surprise 50th birthday that she organised.

Me having a lazy afternoon in the park.

PART TWO

'Awakening is dynamic. Constantly evolving in accordance with life's realities. Unfolding from ego-self to compassionate self. From enclosed self to open self. From foolish self to enlightened self.'

– Taitetsu Unno

7

INTUITION

While I was giving reiki treatments to clients, Ingrid was looking for somewhere for us to live. She found a place called Cemetery Lodge, which was on the grounds of a cemetery. There were four other viewings booked that day, but they all cancelled. The woman showing us around pointed out that one of the rooms would be perfect for a healing room, but she had no idea that we were healers, so we took that as a sign and signed the lease without hesitation.

Ingrid's ex-husband decided to move to England with their children into a house just around the corner from us. He struggled with the idea of their children growing up without their mother, so it seemed like a wonderful compromise to a very emotional situation. However, the reality proved to be very different. Ingrid had expressed to him at one point that she could see us all sitting around the table, being friends and working things out, but he couldn't get over Ingrid leaving, and that was why he really moved to the UK.

Ingrid would be at their house a lot of the time. One of her sons didn't get on well at school, and her ex-husband started behaving aggressively towards Ingrid, so he made the decision, for the sake of his children and his emotional wellbeing, to move back to Belgium with them on Christmas Eve, which was very upsetting for Ingrid.

Since our first meeting in Belgium, Ingrid and I have been told numerous times that we are twin souls and have had many lives together. So even with all the difficulties and the trauma that we have been through, I believe that I was doing what I was led to do, that the universe will reveal what should happen and that it's not up to me to control the outcome. Even if I think from the beginning that something is not going to end well, I will still choose to take the path I have been guided onto. I am here to be of service to the universe. I will not waver from the mission, even when I want to.

We have had 20 hard years as a couple, and I feel as though it's about time that we have some good things happen. We have made a lot of sacrifices, from me losing my house to Sandra, Ingrid crying on weekends because she missed her children, plus the turmoil of moving countries and living in a different culture. At the time of having this book written, Ingrid has been back in Belgium for 12 weeks now, and we have applied for a divorce, but we both still have a lot of love for each other.

I've always found that when you try to change things,

or force things to happen, you might end up banging your head against the wall. The timing of this book being written while Ingrid and I have separated is a great example that we cannot control what happens to us and must trust that all that is happening is part of our life plan. We must embrace it and not question why. Acceptance of things we do not know or want is how we evolve spiritually.

Whatever you want to achieve, you need to put your 50% in and allow the Spirit to put in the other 50%. It is a balance of having trust that the universe will take care of you while simultaneously working with the right energy to enable the right situations to present themselves. It won't be easy. Nothing ever is. But it will happen. I am living proof of that. I'm not interested in wealth, money or accumulation of things. I am interested in the accumulation of experiences.

Cemetery Lodge was a very nice place to live, despite the coming years being very difficult. Ingrid and I knew we had to be together, but being a mother separated from her children was very hard for Ingrid. She struggled with her Catholic upbringing and choosing to go against the traditional way of raising a family. Naturally, she missed them immensely. With all the upsets and stresses we were enduring in the human earthly form, we were equally being rewarded with positive confirmations from our spirit guides that we were doing the right thing.

We knew we had been sent on a mission, and we both had

the same goal. We were doing a lot of spiritual work trying to get our business set up and increase the number of clients we had. We started off doing massages and reiki while also teaching reiki courses. We ended up doing reiki courses all over the country and in Europe, which was wonderful. We fit together perfectly.

I believe that, when I need to make a decision, I have to feel the answer and not think it. Meditation is very useful, and you can try it yourself by sitting quietly for five or 10 minutes and allowing yourself to imagine the outcome of making a decision and experiencing how that makes you feel in the moment.

Imagine there are no self-imposed boundaries and that you are free to do what your instinct is telling you to, and then try and imagine going against your intuition and letting your thoughts and ego take over.

When you make the right choice, positivity will come through, and you will have a feeling of excitement. If it's the wrong decision to make, it will feel like your breath gets taken away. That's coming from your gut; your instinct is kicking in. It is important to note that the right road to take is not always the smoothest, so be mindful of trying to avoid the tests and challenges put in your way, for they are also necessary.

Another approach I take to facing life choices is to ask, 'will it take me closer or further away from my life's purpose?' If I choose not to do what my spirit guides are telling me to do, that decision will take me further away from what I am being asked to do, and that means that I would not be trusting in the universe. You have to have faith in order to fulfil your life's mission.

Moving to Cemetery Lodge is a good example of this. It happened swiftly and easily, and it was meant to be our home. We had about four really happy years there. We used to leave a rock lamp on in our bedroom, and when we'd come home in the evenings, we would come up the driveway past a beautiful big oak tree and could both see the silhouettes of a husband and wife in our bedroom window. Their spirits were caringly waiting for us to come home. They made us feel safe and welcomed.

Me connecting with spirit.

8

CHRIST ENERGY

One of the reasons that Ingrid and I were brought together is because I carry the Christ energy and Ingrid carries the Mary Magdalene energy. Saint Germain brought us together for a specific purpose. On a human level, we're here to bring people together and offer them healing – to open them up and help them see the world differently and to help put people on their spiritual path.

Prior to meeting Ingrid, I went to a healer and she told me she had cleared my crown chakra at the top of my head so that my true self could be revealed because, until then, it had been hidden. I was told, by Ingrid, that I carry the Christ energy and in a previous life, I was Jesus. I couldn't believe that at first.

I was treating an autistic client one day called Mark Bellamy. As I was getting set up, out of nowhere, he looked me straight in the eye and said, 'Steven, I was the Roman soldier who helped you when you were on the cross.' He had language difficulties and struggled to hold a conversation, so there was no obvious explanation as to what would have made him come out with something like that, so for me, that was another confirmation verifying who I was.

Then I had a reading with a medium and she said to me, 'if I didn't know you as Steven, I would think of you as Jesus as I sense His energy within you.' I don't share this knowledge in general conversation because it is quite difficult for me to explain, and people may not understand it.

Jesus, in my personal opinion, was a healer, like me, except he carried a higher frequency of energy and was awakening people on a much larger scale. The higher the frequency of energy you can carry in your body, the more special things you can do. I've had a lot of people tell me that when they have had a healing session with me, they have seen Jesus. It might be hard for some people to understand when I say that I am Jesus, but I'm only a facet or a part of Him. I carry his energy and his energy is love and awakening people to come to love and to raise their consciousness.

I had a past life regression, which is looking back at your previous lives by being put into a hypnotic state, and it came out in that session that I had walked in Jesus's life, and every life prior to that I had been a healer. I obviously can't prove any of this; I am simply retelling what has been told to me.

Simultaneously, Ingrid was told by her spirit guide, Saint Germain, that she carried Mary Magdalene's energy. She is helping to awaken the feminine energy in both men and women and help the feminine energy to rise. The masculine energy has been in control for thousands of years and has done a terrible job of taking care of the Earth, so Ingrid is helping the feminine collective energy to rise and therefore restore balance.

All the different energies of the many lives that you've lived will always be with you. I'm here now as Steven in this life, but I've had many past lives, which help me with my job now. When I perform healings, I have all different people coming through me. When you reincarnate back onto Earth, you don't come down with all your gifts, because if you did, you wouldn't learn anything new. There is and always should be something to learn.

In 2018, Ingrid was woken up at 3 a.m. by Saint Germain, and over the next few nights the same thing happened. He was telling her that we had to go on a spiritual quest to visit all these places in Europe where Jesus and Mary Magdalene had been. We had to visit a lot of castles to balance the energy wherever we went. We didn't have to do anything specific, but just by being there, we were doing something because of the energy that we carry. We had to go to where Mary Magdalene was killed, and where Jesus was buried, and we were guided there by Saint Germain.

We were gone for about five weeks. We had no money to do all of this; being self-employed meant we weren't earning anything while we were away, so it all went on credit cards.

But Ingrid was receiving all of these messages, so we believed that we had to do what we were being told to do.

People said to us, 'Oh, it must have been a lovely holiday,' but it wasn't like that. Through all of the spiritual work we were doing, we were experiencing a lot of internal clearing out as well, and it was hard work that often felt heavy and negative. Plus, I was feeling sorry for myself because I was doing all the driving and we had very little money.

We had to pay for the journey on credit cards. But it's all been paid off, and it's all come back to us since then. You have to show your faith; otherwise, you aren't being tested. When you have been asked to do a six-week trip around Europe with no income or money and have to fill up the car with petrol wondering how it's all going to be paid for, that is showing faith.

We were both going through different things and getting frustrated with each other. But we did the work because Spirit wanted us to do it, and we had some amazing spiritual experiences.

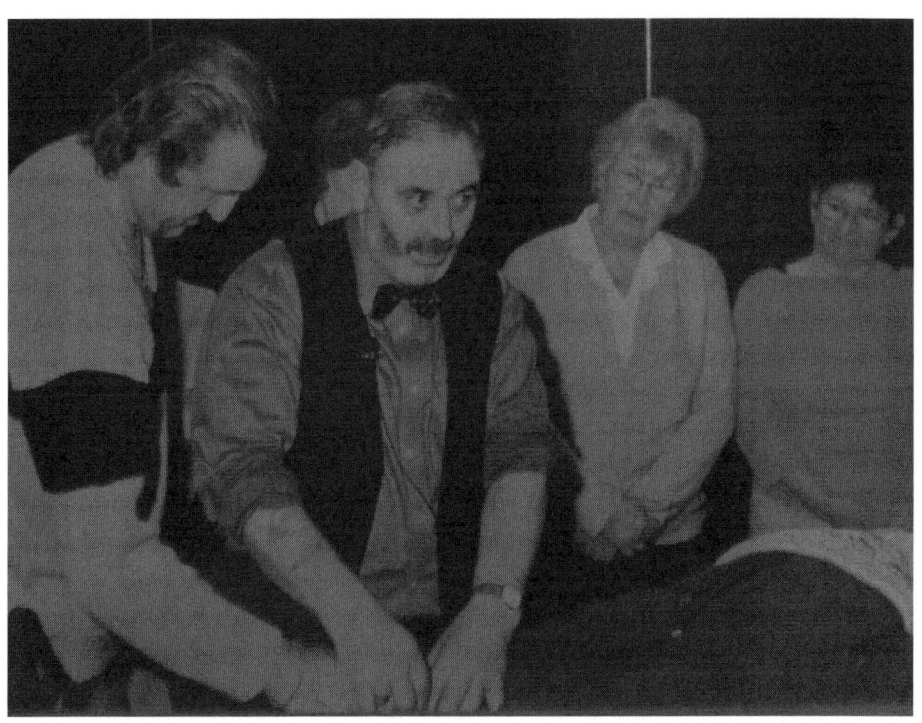

Me working with Ray Brown who is Trancing St Paul, Showing me Knee operation.

9

THE SCHOOL HOUSE

Finding the schoolhouse was a thank you for going on that journey. When we got back from our spiritual tour of Europe, I told Ingrid that we had to sell our house because we needed the money, but we also needed somewhere bigger to grow our business. We always had the dream of running our own retreat and bringing more people to us.

I was searching the internet, looking for something like a barn conversion or even just a bigger house, when this converted school popped up. My initial thought was that the rent wouldn't be affordable, but I wanted to take a look anyway. We came to view it and knew this was our place.

It was a struggle financially during the Covid lockdowns, but we made it through. Now that things are starting to improve, Ingrid and I have separated, and that is part of life's journey. The mission at this point in time is for Ingrid and me to separate everything and, in doing so, restore balance between the male Christ energy and the female Mary Magdalene energy.

On a human level, Ingrid is in Belgium now to create something like this retreat over there while I carry on my work here. But also, on a spiritual level, by her being there and me being here, it is another way of separating the two energies (male and female), with the purpose of preparing those two energies to be able to come back together at a later time, when it is necessary.

There is a shift happening from all the years of the feminine energy being suppressed, which is now rising, and we can see this happening around the world, where more women are in top positions in government and big companies. So we are helping everyone behind us to rise with this change in energy.

I feel that I am balanced with male and female energy, so as a man, I don't feel threatened by the shift that is happening. I observe how a lot of men behave, how some can be very opinionated and uncaring. My dad is an example of an older generation who doesn't respect people of different races for example and doesn't seem to even respect himself. So I can see that a lot of men need to get in touch with their feminine side.

If you have too much of the male energy in you, then you will have a big problem with the change; it will unnerve you. When I have male clients come here, I talk to them about balancing their feminine side and, with enough understanding, they realise the importance of creating harmony.

Terra Nova School Of Light, our retreat centre and home.

Me receiving an award from the I.C.N.M for Highly Commended Practitioner for work with Autism.

Giving a talk on treating Autism to Reiki Federation UK.

10

OUR PURPOSE

A few years ago, when Ingrid and I were at the height of our spiritual journey and awakening, we had received strong messages that we needed to go to Ireland. We booked a trip with the premise of looking for a place to live and set up business. We stayed in a lovely cottage right on the sea. As soon as Ingrid walked into the place, she said she couldn't breathe and couldn't stay there. Exhausted from driving all day, I didn't know what to do. A few hours later, I went to the bedroom to lie down, and spirits started coming to me, begging for help.

I received a vision that I needed to go to the beach, five minutes from the cottage. On the beach, there was a Celtic cross, where I needed to open a portal. The following day, Ingrid and I went to perform a ceremony, which were repeated words of affirmations: 'I am here, opening this portal of light to release all these spirits to find peace and love.' It felt as though they were all trapped. It turned out that they had died tragic deaths due to the potato famine and as a result, their spirits hadn't moved on. That was the reason for our journey; we were not meant to live there after all.

What I did was heavy on my body and incredibly emotional. I asked my spirit guides why had they sent me there to do that. The message I received back was, if I had known the real reason and the cost of it, I may not have gone and that would have interfered with the universal law of what needed to be done.

The messages are always presented in a way for me to act upon whatever I am asked to do. No matter how difficult it may be, I always go back to asking the same question: 'Will this take me closer to my life's purpose or further away?' Whatever message you get, don't question it. Have confidence in your intuition, and don't hesitate to act. Just do what you are being asked.

We are not separate from the spirit world. Just because you can't see your spirit guide beside you doesn't mean they are not there. It's like the wind: you can feel it on your face, but you can't see it. Talking with your spirit guide is no different than talking with a loved one.

When I asked my spirit guides why I was still working in butchery instead of being a healer full-time, I was told I was meant to help people who were not yet awakened and plant seeds within them. Between my healing work, running reiki workshops, going through the butchery training assessments and all the paperwork that entailed, I was busy seven days a week. I was doing that for about 10 years while Ingrid and I were building up this retreat. It wasn't a straight path of swapping one profession for another. We had to build our business and reputation through word of mouth before we were comfortably able to commit to it full-time, which took a long time.

Just came out of Sweet Lodge where we released Spirits that had been trapped.
Left to right Ingrid, Hannah and me.

Having a blessing from my spiritual guide in the highlands of Scotland.

Teaching Reiki to a group at Mountain Thyme in Asheville North Carolina America.

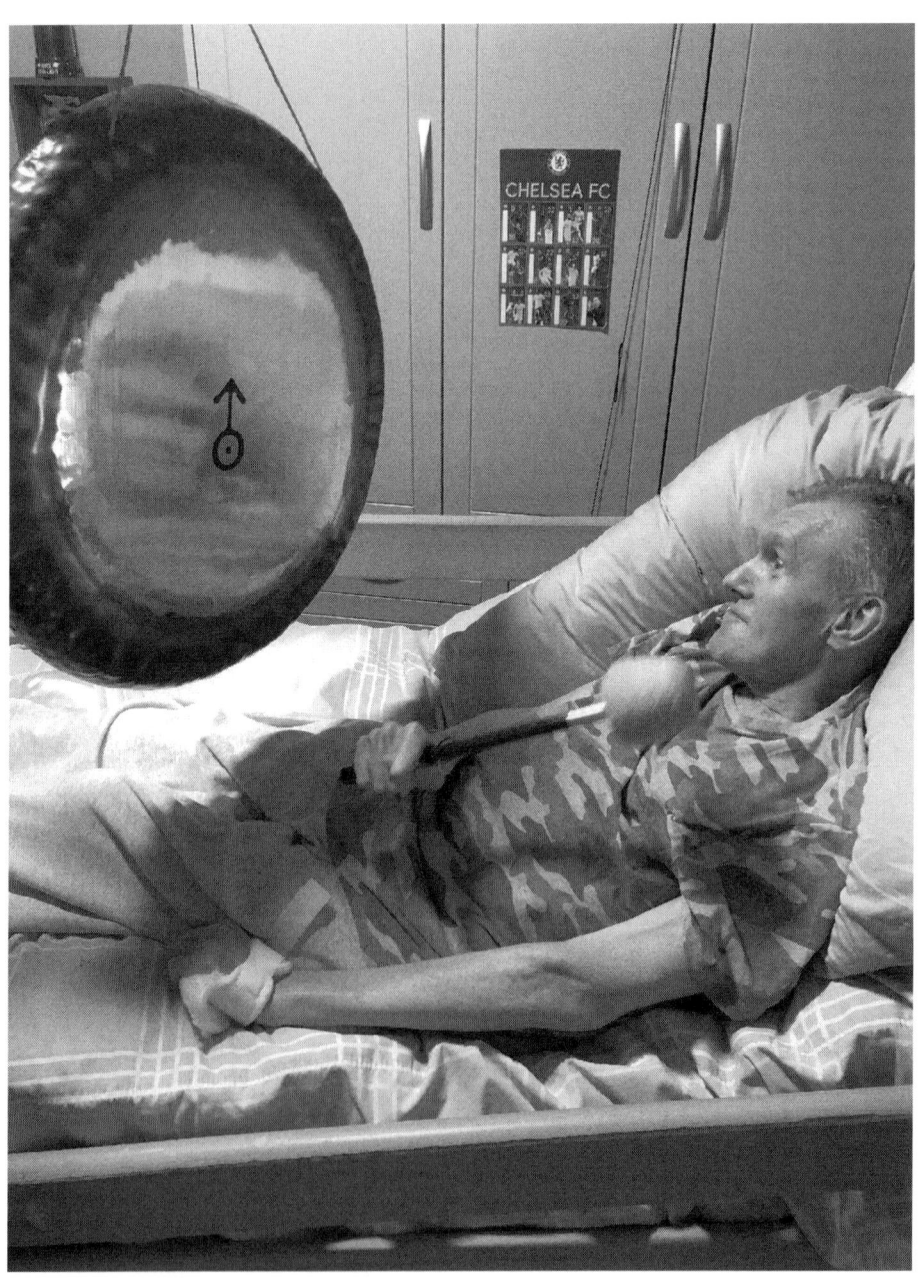

Me treating one of my clients with sound therapy in their support home.

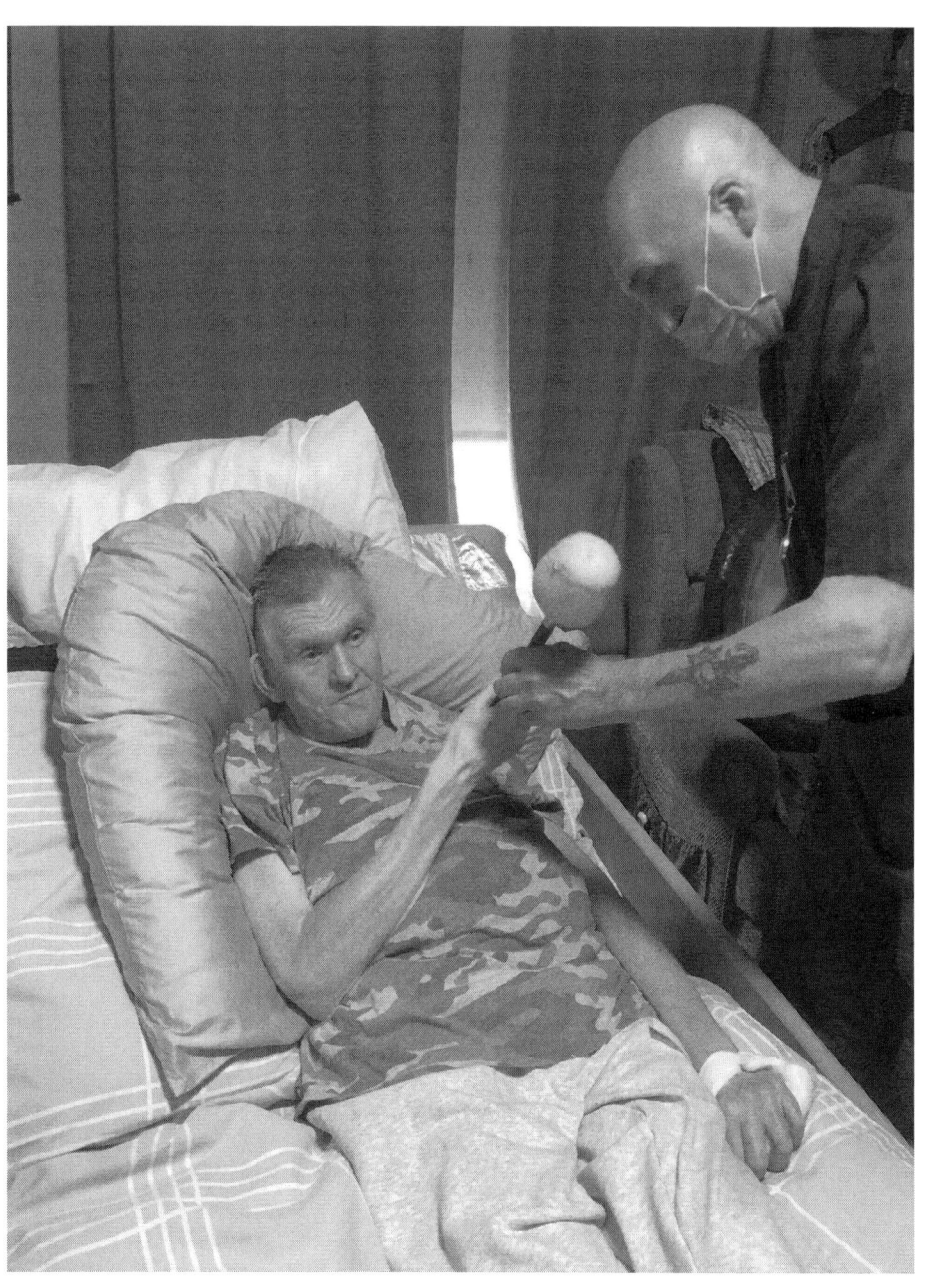

Me and John on one of his Sound therapy session.

Me and Harry, one of my butchery students who won the award for the most achieved student who had overcome difficulties.

11

OUR SACRED JOURNEY

by Ingrid and Steven Rudelhoff, 2018

Ingrid

One night in May of this year, I was woken up at 3 am by my beautiful spiritual guide St Germain. He asked me to sit in front of the computer and start planning a journey, a spiritual quest. I had been thinking about going to Belgium for my mum's and daughter's birthday, so he told me to start the trip in Belgium first. When we visited my family last time, we stayed in a very magical cottage called "Brechts Boshuisje". I looked it up online and it was still available for our time period, so I was told to book it.

Steven and I had been talking for a while to go back to the South of France as we feel very much at home there. St

Germain told me that that would be our next stop and guided me to the right website and the right gite to hire. The gite was called Gite Fleuri (translated: the flower gite), based in the Cathar village of Limousis, Aude, north of Carcassonne. Again, the gite was available for the time period we needed to stay there, so I was told to book it.

Then I asked St Germain where we had to go next. He said, Switzerland. Earlier in the year, he had mentioned a trip to Switzerland to me, to the region of Wengen. When I looked up accommodation in that area, I found a 300-year-old wooden farm cottage, facing the Jungfrau mountain peak. That holiday letting was fully booked except for the week that we needed to go there … so I was told to book it.

From Switzerland we were to travel to Germany, where we had already booked a stay in Osterronfeld to visit both the Paiste and Oetken gong factories. I had to change the accommodation as Mini, our beautiful "dragon" greyhound was to come with us on this special journey and the hotel accommodation would not suit her. I found a pet-friendly Airbnb studio in the house of Tony, an Englishman who lives in Blumenthal (translated: valley of the flowers), about 20 minutes away from the factories…

In the morning, I shared this information with Steven and he was very excited with the whole project. Then came the hardest part; how were we to finance this trip? We didn't have the money readily available and being self-employed, this would mean 5 weeks without any income … We meditated on it and did our oracle cards. All the messages we received were saying that we had to do this journey to allow a new chapter in our lives of service to Spirit to unfold. We followed St Germain's motto *"Act as if you have already got it"* and we booked all the accommodations and travel arrangements, using a credit card. We have done this in the past, trusting that we would be reimbursed in some way. However, this time we were faced with the biggest expense ever … Still confronted with human doubt, we decided to go to spiritualist church and through the medium, we received messages from our loved ones in spirit, confirming to make this bold move. On the way to church, I asked St Germain to give me a sign and he showed me himself sitting on a throne in the clouds, watching over me.

Before we left for Belgium, Steven felt a strong need to go and see his parents and tell them about the journey and why we had to do it, facing his dad's fears related to money. Both his parents embraced the idea fully and were very excited about the trip.

Our stay in Belgium was magical. My parents also embraced our trip fully as well as the thought of us re-locating to the South of France. The most beautiful thing that happened during our Belgian stay was the fact that – for the first time in 14 years - both of my children wanted to know my part of the story related to me leaving their dad and consequently accepted Steven for who he truly is and why I am with him. We had the most amazing conversations with them about spiritual subjects and about our sacred journey as well as why Steven and I are together. I also attuned my son and his wife to Reiki and passed on some of the Munay Ki rites to them, enabling them to move forward on their paths. I passed on the powerful 13th Rite of Munay Ki, the Rite of the Womb, to my daughter and her friend to help them release their fears and move forward on their life's journeys.

Then we started the second leg of our special trip: the South of France. The region we were going to – the stunning Cathar land - is connected to very significant past lives and I was told by St Germain which power places to visit and what to do there.

I was also shown a plot of land for sale on a website. We arranged a viewing and when we went there, we both knew that we belonged on that plot of land.

We received extra signs about this, such as the number of the plot – 77 – which in numerology is the number 5. This number is our numerology number and it keeps returning to us on important occasions. The road leading to the plot is the D509, which makes the number 5 again. Later on that day, we walked around Limousis, the hamlet in which we were staying. During our walk, we discussed the viewing and the fact that we should be living in that area. The number 5 returned on the building date of the church in Limousis – 1661 ...

After viewing the plot of land, we went to the mystical Pech de Bugarach nearby, a mountain peak known for its connection to the Lemurian and Atlantic civilisations. Driving to the mountain peak, I had a vision of myself, traveling down that same road, but the road was a dusty sand road and I was on horseback, dressed in leather, accompanied by other men on horseback. We were knights and we were laughing and joking about something. As I mentioned this to Steven whilst in the car, he said that at exactly the same time, he felt a pressure on his head, like he was wearing a helmet… When we came back from visiting that mountain, we both felt light-headed and felt like we had been connected to the energy of the Bugarach mountain.

As instructed by St Germain, I booked the viewing of the land for the 5th of September. In its entirety - 05-09-2018 - this date forms the number 7, the holy number, spiritually representing the foundation of God's word and God's creation of things: 7 days of the week, 7 organs of the body, 7 planets, 7 chakras, 7 elements of alchemy… I did feel that this land coming our way was part of God's plan…

The previous day, we visited a local cave – *la Grotte de Limousis*. During the visit, we entered the "Music Room", one of the halls in the cave where the locals used to come to have celebrations and play music. I asked the guide if it would be possible to do some gong playing in the cave. "Of course,", he replied, "When would you like to come?"

So we went back that same afternoon and took the Sound

Creation Earth Gong, to give healing and thanks to the Earth and to the Cave. It was absolutely magical!!! (See video clip on our website in the Sound Healing section)

As mentioned previously, before leaving on our sacred journey, St Germain guided me to certain websites and information about specific power places in Cathar land, that we needed to touch to heal significant past lives.

On Friday 07-09-2018, which makes the number 9, we had to go on the trail of Jesus and Mary Magdalene and visit the places where they were buried. For Jesus that is Roc Redon, near the hamlet of Opoul-Perillos.

St Germain, who was Joseph of Arimathea in the life of Jesus, told me that he and Jesus were heading towards a shipment in the harbour of Port Leucate when they came under siege by Roman soldiers and were killed. The Lord of the Chateau of Perillos at that time had his men carry the bodies up to the castle to have them prepared for burial. They then buried the bodies in rock tombs on the powerful Roc Redon …. We couldn't climb Roc Redon so Steven did a ritual by an olive tree, standing below the castle grounds and facing Roc Redon. [Doing some research on this area afterwards, I found that the plateau on which the chateau stands is called Terre Salvayre which means, Land of the Saviour, or Salveterra in Occitan.]

After having done that ritual, we then had to go to the burial place of Mary Magdalene, near Rennes-le-Chateau. Because of being highly pregnant with their second child

– a boy – Mary did not accompany her husband Jesus and Joseph of Arimathea to the sea. She was sieged and killed by Roman soldiers on a rocky hill slope facing Rennes-le-Chateau (meaning "Queen of the Chateau", representing Mother Earth). They cut open her belly, took out her unborn son and killed him in front of her eyes. Then they threw her off the rocks. The locals buried her and her son in the cave underneath the precipice, called *"la Grotte du Fournet"*. I did a ritual to clear and heal that trauma by an olive tree in-between the Magdala Tower of Rennes-le-Chateau and the cave.

After having performed both rituals, we then had to go to Rennes-les-Bains (meaning "Queen of the Water", representing Mother Moon) for cleansing.

When I looked up the spiritual meaning of number 9, I found that it represents the completion of the Divine plan and being of Divine service. It also conveys a meaning of finality.

St Germain also asked to go to certain of the Cathar castles, related to the life of King Arthur and his Templar knights. We already passed two of them on our ritual track, namely the Chateau d'Aguilar and the Chateau de Termes.

On September 11, 2018, alongside the Chateau of Montsegur, we also visited the Chateau de Queribus, the Chateau de Puilaurens and the Chateau de Peyrepertuse, which - together with the Chateau d'Aguilar and the Chateau de Termes – are called the "Five Sons of Carcassonne".

All of them are connected to the Old Castle City of Carcassonne and the Chateau de Montsegur (see above) and were visited by King Arthur and his knights Templar to assist them in times of war and to hold secret rituals in.

We both felt very tired, but very empowered at the same time after finishing our tour of these castles. Looking up the spiritual meaning of the number 4 – formed by the date 11-09-2018 – I found that it means 'God setting all the things in order', connecting mind-body-spirit with the physical world of structure and organisation. The number 4 represents the safety and security of home, the need for stability and strength on a solid foundation of values and beliefs. That is exactly what those power places represented then and still do to this day and beyond... Visiting them, we took the energies needed to build a new place in this area, where people can be empowered to re-construct the foundation of old values and beliefs.

Despite the fact that all of our experiences had been magical so far, we were continuously under attack of negativity in the form of negative thoughts, self-doubt, fear … trying to stop us from doing this quest and trying to make us feel unworthy of a life here. This links in with a third and vital reason why we had to do this journey: other than re-visiting and healing past lives, we also had to balance the masculine and the feminine energies, both within ourselves and within our relationship, this by letting go of all fears and barriers still within us.

All throughout our stay in France, we were visited by these beautiful black-and-white butterflies, which we called the yin-and-yang butterflies, who were there to heal us, to balance the masculine and the feminine energies and to show us the way to inner peace and unconditional love.

Having visited all these power sites and having done all our rituals, our light was shining stronger and we were feeling more and more empowered. That also meant that we were more and more under siege of negativity. For example: two days before leaving France and getting ready for our next leg of the journey – i.e., Switzerland - we were going on a short trip out to Hautpoul, a medieval village nearby Mazamet. It was only about 45 minutes away from our gite and we planned to be back mid-afternoon. The village was magical, especially the luminous dragonfly that visited us while walking around the medieval garden and stayed with us for over 10 minutes, telling us to believe in the magic of nature and the universe. It would not go away. In the end, we had to leave it behind in the garden because of wasps pestering us...

On the way back, driving through beautiful forest on the Montagne Noire (Black Mountain) and passing through little hamlets, we were blocked in one hamlet by a car with its wheel arch stuck in the wall of a house, thus blocking the road while desperately trying to get unstuck, holding up all the traffic. Straightaway did I feel that this was another play of the negativity trying to attack us as this meant having to reverse and make a detour, driving another extra hour on top of the return journey. This made a late return home and both of us feeling exhausted and fed up, especially after all the previous driving we had been doing ... I sat outside in the courtyard and felt this wave of self-doubt come over me, questioning everything: Why did we have to do this trip? Did we really want to live here, in the mountains with windy, narrow roads? How will we be able to afford making this move?... All of a sudden, I was aware of my beautiful guide sitting in the chair opposite me. He gave me a number of the angel number book – number 156 – which read: *All your material needs are supplied as you take the human steps necessary to commence the changes you've been guided to make. Keep your thoughts positive about these changes.* It felt like he was saying these words to me instead of me reading them in the book. I was also aware that coming closer to our next leg of the journey, the negativity was trying to stop us from going to Switzerland. That night I had a dream, in which I was served a big red lobster in a restaurant. When I read up on the symbolic meaning of this dream, I found the following explanation: *lobster brings you strength. You can overcome all challenges with persistence. It signifies profit and reward that comes from standing your own ground and overcoming your difficulties and problems.* When I did my oracle cards that next morning, all these were validating our journey and transition, which made me feel positive again about going to Switzerland.

We arrived in Switzerland on Saturday 15-09-2018. We

strongly felt that our leg in Belgium and in France had been preparations for the proper vision quest to take place on the Swiss mountain top. The Alpenhutte, in which we were staying, was placed opposite the Jungfrau mountain peak and was located next to a huge waterfall. Together with the elements of air (wind) and fire (sun) – both earth (mountain) and water (waterfall) gave us instant healing and balance when we arrived there after a 12-hour-trip. We felt re-energized on the spot.

Looking at the date of arrival, I noticed that it represented the number 8, the number that stands for abundance, but also for balance of both material and spiritual aspects. I was told by St Germain that this visit would set us on our further path, both in a spiritual and a material way, which linked in with the biblical meaning of number 8 – i.e., new beginning, new order or creation.

The lemniscate or figure of 8 is also the symbol of eternity.

The first night in the Alpenhutte, I linked in with the energy of the Jungfrau Mountain before going to sleep. *Jungfrau* means young maiden in English. When I closed my eyes, I saw a beautiful young woman with a very serene and pure face and very warm, gentle, brown eyes. She welcomed me to the mountain peak and gave me a very loving, warm embrace. Later that night, in my dream, I was taken back to my student years at the university. Together with two male fellow students, we stood in front of a table, behind which a man was seated, who was telling us about a test we were about to take, a physical test. We had to sit in some kind of bobsleigh, with me in the middle, and we would be paintsprayed along the ride. The three colours of paint were the primal colours: red – yellow – blue. We were given goggles to protect our eyes and a mask to protect our nose and mouth. The man told me that I had done this test before, but didn't fully pass, so I had to do it again … When I came back from the ride, I saw that I was sprayed in red – primal red. When I woke up, I remembered my dream and looked up the red over red bottle in the Aura-Soma book. It was bottle number 6 (the Alpenhutte was house number 6 …) and the message it gave was that I needed to be re-energised with vital energy and to be healed of resentment, frustration or even anger, which I had been feeling lately about certain situations in my life.

Having arrived safely in Switzerland didn't mean the end of negative attacks. As our lights were becoming even more brighter after our previous empowerments in the South of France, the darkness would come to us even more and quite unexpectedly … This time it was through our greyhound Mini. On the Sunday, during a walk, Mini – on her lead – got shocked by an electric fence wire and Steven had to grasp her and hold her down for dear life or she would have run off in a panic. As a result, he got bitten by Mini all over his head … Luckily, we were able to calm her down and bring her back to the cabin in one piece. The next day, she got hold of her collar and chewed it in two … Luckily we found a new collar in a pet shop not too far away – a red one with white crosses on, representing the Swiss flag. Looking up the Aura-Soma combination of red and white, I found bottle number 55 – The Christ – the energy to work with and for the light; a bottle related to the test that is indicative of whether or not someone is able to take on spiritual responsibility, very much representing the goal of our vision quest ... This bottle is used to let go of anger, frustration and resentment within through allowing emotional release and showing sacrificial love, like Christ did on the cross. After receiving this message, Steven and I did a ritual, invoking the Violet Flame, to cleanse ourselves of all the negativity we were feeling – especially frustration.

Later that day, I did some reading in a book on the Cathar belief system. They believed in two Gods, one good and one bad one – i.e., the light and the dark. It said that the more you embrace your dark side, the more you will release it and eventually you will not be affected by the bad God anymore.

I must have continued to do this subconsciously throughout the night, which lead to a true revelation the next morning – i.e., Tuesday 18-09-2018.

I went to bed that night and before going to sleep I did some healing on myself, connecting to the energy of the Jungfrau. She told me to place my hands on my heart and on my solar plexus. As I did this, I could feel liquid gold flowing out of my hands into my solar plexus and into my heart. It felt very soothing. Then I went to sleep. In my dream, I encountered the Jungfrau again. This time she was a resident in a care home with young adults with emotional issues. I complimented her on how beautiful she looked inside as well as outside.

When I woke up on Tuesday morning, I connected with the mountain again and again she told me to place my hands on my solar plexus and to connect with the essence of the liquid gold. Then she told me to visualise the liquid gold covering the insides of my body. It felt amazing!

I got up and did my Aura-Soma card of the day. When I put that one back, I was drawn to another one, referring to bottle 0 – the bottle of the spiritual rescue. Its tarot card is called The Fool on the outward journey. When I saw its picture, the revelation came: a man, dressed in gold, is unaware that he is stepping off a cliff while following a butterfly. There is a huge mountain in the background, resembling the Jungfrau. When I saw the gold, the following insight came to me: "We don't need to make or find the gold; we are the gold. Connect to the essence of liquid gold and let it fill the whole of your body, so you become liquid gold and everything you touch becomes gold too." That man represented Steven and myself, chasing our dream of transformation and while doing so, jumping off a cliff to release ourselves of all human fear, frustration, resentment, anger ... That tarot card referred to new possibilities coming our way to reach our full potential, inviting us to be open to wisdom from beyond and to follow our inner child excitement.

I could take all of those messages, thanked all of nature – those beautiful wisdomkeepers – for their guidance and for sharing their wisdom with us.

When I looked up the meaning of Bottle 0, my eye also fell on the next page of the book, showing Bottle 1 – the bottle of physical rescue, which we have. I knew we both had to put that on us as it would help us with letting go of all negativity, all difficulties of the past and a feeling of unworthiness – which we both still struggled with. When looking up its meaning in the tarot card book, I was struck by its picture. It shows the Magician and the land where he stands is an exact reflection of the land we want to live and work on in France ... All of the symbols in the picture made perfect sense to me and were all connected to our dream life. The messages of the card made perfect sense too, stating that we are fully equipped and ready to go, that we are aligning ourselves to become a connection between heaven and earth, by using the tools in life, which we have developed through training, life experience and spiritual connection. Basically, it was saying that we had graduated!

I cried out of sheer happiness and relief that we found the answers that we came for and expressed my love and my gratitude to all of the wisdomkeepers and enlightened beings around us! THANK YOU LIFE!!!

Looking at the date, I realised that it made number 2, so I looked up the symbolic meaning of number 2: it stands for the Divine Feminine and for harmony. It seeks to end separateness and unite all for the greater good. In its biblical sense, it stands for unity and confirms that there is another. I felt that this very strongly related to harmony within our twin soul relationship.

As a cleansing and celebration of this epiphany, Steven and I had a bath in the outdoor hot tub.

On Wednesday 19-09-2018, I felt emotionally "wobbly". When I picked my Aura-Soma card of the day, I picked the bottle 22 card, the yellow over pink, which relates to a renewal of spirit through joy and self-acceptance; to love the self unconditionally and to have a new perspective on life; letting go of fear and anxiety, thus finding the complete you and experiencing true love. The tarot reading related to this card talks shows the Fool (see bottle 0 explanation above) but on the return journey. Bottle 22 is also called the Rebirth bottle, where the Fool has found himself. On the picture he is dressed in gold (yellow) with pink roses of unconditional love blooming all around him. This card represents the aha-moment. He is now enlightened, following spirit without fear or physical distraction. He is in love with life.

When I looked at my "union jack flag" dress, which Freddie Mercury asked me to wear on our visit to his studio in Montreux, I noticed that it has yellow over pink on it: yellow heart-shaped glasses over a pink crown ...

Indeed, one of the other reasons we had to be in this area of Switzerland was to be able to visit Montreux and

The Studio Experience of the rock band Queen. Ever since Steven and I got together, Freddie Mercury has been guiding us on our spiritual path, supporting us all the way.

We visited the studio on Wednesday 19-09-2018, number 3 in numerology. Freddie guided us all the way to the studio, arranged for a parking space about 2 minutes' walk away and made sure that there were hardly any other visitors there. We could even take Mini – our greyhound – with us as it was too hot to keep her in the car and she felt uneasy staying in the hut on her own. As soon as we entered the exhibition hall, we could feel Freddie's presence, his essence. I did have my picture taken by his statue - as promised - holding open the union jack flag of my dress, demonstrating his love for Britain and for the Queen.

All along that day, we felt under attack again. Freddie told me to hang in there as we were almost there! He also told me that things would appear on the pictures that Steven was taking

There was no one else in the recording studio when Steven took this picture... Notice Freddie standing on the right as well as St Germain's shadow next to Steven.

Going back to the date we visited the studio and to its numerology number 3, this number symbolises the power of three and the tripartide nature of the world: heaven, earth and waters. I feel that this relates to the album "Made in Heaven", dedicated to Freddie's immortal memory and which is all about the connection between heaven and earth, made next to the beautiful waters of Lac Leman. The number 3 also relates to the human being as being body, soul and spirit in one; the coming together of the physical and the spiritual. Number 3 is the number of manifesting and manifestation and carries the vibration of the Ascended Masters. In the Bible, the number 3 was used to put a divine stamp of completion or fulfilment on the subject. When Steven asked me to stand somewhere for a picture, I intuitively went to stand next to the "Made In Heaven" cabinet ...

Later that night, Freddie gave me Aura-Soma bottle 45 in the tarot book – called Breath of Love.

The bottle itself is made of my main energy colours: turquoise and magenta. When I looked at the picture and read the explanation, I realised that it was an illustration of who Freddie is and what Freddie did for us that day: *A heavenly soul oversees a joyful scene, blowing kisses with her breath of love. The cups are filled with delight, music, flowers, abundance, surprises and innocent happiness. Joy and intuition (the sixth sense) find room for expression within the contented community.*

And that is exactly what he did to us – blowing unconditional love over us, thus helping us to release the remainder of sadness and pain that we were still carrying. He made us feel care-free and filled with unconditional love!

Thank you, Freddie, for an amazing experience, for always supporting us and for being there when we need you the most!!!

On Thursday 20-09-18, I woke up feeling light. So did

Steven. Something had shifted! I picked an Aura-Soma card and it was bottle 98, the bottle of Archangel Sandalphon, related to someone in the process of change with the gift of unconditional love to help him/her through this. The message on the tarot card suggests how you can be healed and transformed through love, but you need to be the one to give it!

Thursday's date made the number 4. We have had eagles visit us daily during our stay in the Alphutte. On Thursday, there were 4 (!) circling over us when we sat outside. I looked up the symbolic meaning of number 4: it represents the four elements (air, fire, water and earth) and the four directions. It also resonates with the energies of the Archangels (hence Archangel Sandalphon in the card reading). In numerology it is connected with hard work and completeness. In the Bible, it symbolises God setting all the things in order. In Munay Ki, eagle/condor is the archetype related to the heart chakra, helping us to see the bigger picture. *He reminds you to take heart and gather your courage, for the universe is presenting you with an opportunity to soar above the mundane levels of your life. The power of recognizing this opportunity may come in the form of a spiritual test. In being astute, you may recognise the places within your soul, personality, emotions, or psyche that need bolstering or refinement. By looking at the overall tapestry, eagle teaches you to broaden your sense of self beyond the horizon of what is presently visible...* (from *Medicine Cards* by Jamie Sams and David Carson).

I felt that we passed our test!

Later on that night, for cleansing and celebrating, we had a bath in the outdoor hot tub, under the stars and looking at the Moon, Mars and Saturn.

Reading up on the significance and meaning of both planets, it fitted the picture perfectly – Saturn bringing us stability and perseverance to carry on our spiritual pathway; Mars guiding us to passion, self-mastery and rightly steering our energies to further our goal. Looking into my Moon diary, I came across the section Monthly Forecast for September 2018 and read how after the New Moon on September 9, deep-seated toxins would come to light, focusing particular attention on issues of wealth and power, and how all relationships would feel the tension, which would grow until September 20 (being that day), with some of them possibly snapping under the strain... We definitely felt it the days leading up to that date!

In the night of Thursday 20 to Friday 21 September, I woke up – feeling a shock going through my body and a heaviness on my upper chest. At first, I thought I was having a panic attack, which has happened in the past after a period of intense mental-emotional stress. When focusing upon the area of discomfort - I also felt it in my back at the same height – I was told that my high heart chakra was being opened up. I found an interesting website (basmati. com) which explained that the high heart brings together the consciousness and the signatures of the heart and the throat chakra in a beautiful, harmonious, powerful way. This chakra is all about living your personal truth and doing so with passion and conviction. Working on the high heart center can put you into greater alignment with your "cosmic mission" and help you come into more harmonious relationships and create soul agreements with others, which serves the greater whole. The website also mentioned that you can open up your high heart chakra with rose water. Interestingly enough, I used rose water on my upper chest area before going to bed to relieve my skin from sunburn …

My beautiful guide St Germain also gave me a number from our Angel Number book (by Doreen Virtue) - number 167: *It's important for you to acknowledge yourself for your accomplishments. Pat yourself on the back and know that you're infinitely loved and appreciated by the Universe. Spirit is ensuring you that all your material needs are supplied today and tomorrow.*

When doing my daily Aura-Soma card, I picked bottle 12, called "Peace in the New Aeon", which tuned in perfectly with my nightly experience, mentioning this new time in our lives to be a time of both trial and initiation, where we are supported by our faith and increasing wisdom, giving us a new perspective on life, still feeling a little disoriented while adjusting to a new reality. When I shared this with Steven, he said that that was exactly how he felt …

On Monday 24 and Tuesday 25 September, we visited several gongmakers in Germany.

When we visited the first one – Gongland – Steven felt

very drawn to the Silent Peace gong.

When we visited the last one – Paiste – I felt very drawn to the Mars Planet gong. The planet Mars had been significantly present during our stay in Switzerland. When I read up on this planet gong, it made perfect sense: *The Mars tones will help you to build and accomplish your earthly, spiritual and physical goals. It will help you to marshal and direct your energy. It is the Gong of decisive self mastery and courage. Low self-esteem and anxiety disappear under its masculine vibrations.* This gong is going to help us and the people coming to us for guidance.

While at Paiste, we were also drawn to another planet gong – the Earth Sidereal Day gong: *This gong provides you with the balance to be able to complete your destiny successfully. It can be used to dislodge suppressed emotions or energy blocks. It focuses you and concentrates the mind ready to face the day. Key words: creativity, youth, birth, wisdom, vitality, freedom, nature and a reason for being.* Again, another useful tool to use! Not once did we question our decision to purchase these gongs! We just knew they had to be with us.

On the way back to England, I was sitting in the car when my guide told me to pay attention to certain numbers on number plates of cars in front of us or overtaking us. He would tell me when to write down the numbers and told me that they corresponded with a number in the Angel Number book. When looking the numbers up, I came to the following resume:

You have to focus on your desires, not your fears. Pay attention to repetitive thoughts as they are messages from above. The Ascended Masters are working with you. A gateway has opened for you and your thoughts are quickly manifesting into reality. Congratulations as you have listened to your intuition and rewards are coming your way. You will be helping others as a result. Be optimistic about your future. Heaven is giving you a new windfall of abundance and a major positive life change. Thousands of angels surround you. All is well! Miracles and new opportunities are coming your way, so focus on your life mission now as it is needed in the world and your preparation is complete. Only hold positive thoughts and expectations about material issues. Rest assured that all your material needs are met. Your thoughts are manifesting quickly, so fully embark on your sacred mission!

After the ceremony I did in Switzerland opposite the Jungfrau.

Playing Sound Creation Earth gong in a cave in the South France on our vision quest.

PART THREE

'The spiritual journey is the unlearning of fear and the acceptance of love.'

– Marianne Williamson

12

LIFE LESSONS

If you are reading this book and you want a self-help guide to achieving, manifesting and changing your life, these are some of the things I would advise.

First of all, you are the creator of your own life. Even if you're having a really dark day or going through challenging times, we all have the ability to change the story of our lives. You need to have confidence and faith in what you do and what you believe in. Don't let anyone tell you otherwise. Believe in your gut feeling. Don't think about what you are feeling; simply allow yourself to *feel*. Read books and seek advice from other mentors. Whatever you do, it has to feel right. If it doesn't feel right, then it isn't.

Changing your life is not easy. There's no magic wand that will make all of your problems disappear. You are here to learn lessons. By going through difficult challenges, we are brought closer to our divine self. Our Divine Nature is leading us to the answers. What we are learning is how to love on a deeper level. No matter what is happening to us, we've got to accept it and radiate that love.

If you are unable to tap into that part of yourself because you perhaps live in a negative state, I suggest you start just by changing one room in your home. Move a bit of furniture around, burn some incense or sit in silence and try to go within and feel your internal self, hear your internal voice.

I would also suggest changing the colours of your clothes because all colours represent different energies. If you're in a negative state, which is a lower vibration, we need to elevate from that, so try wearing some bright colours. There's nothing wrong with wearing black, but you want to be uplifted. Try to do something that you wouldn't normally do. Take a different route on a regular walk or get out in nature more.

An exercise I use with my students in learning how to let go of fear is to start with something small and build on that. For example, jumping off a little step with the intention of letting go of things that are holding them back. Start with small, subtle changes and don't look for the big a-ha moment. There will be no fireworks and bangs. Change in your life takes time. It takes hard work and commitment, and there are plenty of people around that are willing to help you with all of that.

Trying not to worry is one of the biggest challenges. Let go of worry and trust that in this life, you will be helped when you need it, but that may not happen exactly when you ask for it. There is another world out there. We can die a physical death, but our spirit will still carry on. Let go of control, and allow the universe take over.

Believe in yourself; don't follow the crowd. Be different. Be the special person you are here to be. Specialness and peace starts from within, not from the outside world. Manifesting is practising affirmations to change your life. It's like a domino effect: the affirmations that you say start to be created.

If we're dealing with a person who has a lot of anxiety and is fearful, they have given their power away. So a good affirmation to use there would be, 'I take back my power. I am strong. I am powerful. I'm not going to be fearful any more.' When it comes to energy, we are all vibrations, so if we keep repeating these words, it will increase our vibration, and this will give us back our power.

If you don't feel comfortable saying affirmations, you can write down what you want. For example, you might write, 'I want to be happy, and I want to be in control of my life.' Then safely burn that piece of paper with the belief and intention that what you have written is going up to the universe and is manifesting. Just making that conscious decision that you are going to change your life and you are not going to be fearful anymore will cause a shift in your circumstances.

We all go through difficult situations and can fall into the trap of saying: 'Why is this happening to me? I don't deserve this. I've been good all my life. I've worked hard all of my life.' Instead, turn it around and look for things to be grateful for, such as saying: 'The sky is beautiful today' or 'I'm warm and safe in my house.' Find the things that you're thankful for and be appreciative and grateful.

Showing thanks can be very simple, such as getting in bed at night and thanking your body for the organs and blood being pumped that keeps you alive. Just by saying these words and believing them, you are sending healing thoughts and energy through your body. By giving gratitude and thanks, you are creating a loving energy that allows you to blossom. There are so many things happening every day within our body and our energy fields that we don't see. We only see what the mind wants us to.

Before working with energy, I was a hothead. My dad always told me to hit first and ask questions later. After being bullied all the time and being called names, I used to get very angry. But as soon as I started working with energy, it felt like the fire had gone out of my anger. It made me more at peace. Through this work, I have become more sensitive, so I can sense what's going on around the world, including anger and fear.

It's important for people to ask themselves, when they do get angry and frustrated, if it's their anger they're feeling or the anger of the collective? Most of the time, we are absorbing external anger, which we interpret as our own. We need to be more self-aware to understand the difference. As soon as you know the anger is not yours, it goes away.

You only feel anger when you think about it; it's your thoughts that control it. You start thinking about the things someone has done to upset you, which sets off a chemical reaction of emotions. When my own anger rises, which it has done over the last couple of weeks because of what is going on with myself and Ingrid, I use my affirmations and think about the positive things I will be doing that day or week to move my thoughts away from anger. I am able to change my mood and turn it around.

It's good to feel anger. You don't want to suppress it. It's about controlling the way you let it out. You can do that by taking deep breaths. With your inward breath, bring in nice, beautiful thoughts. Breathe out the bad, the anger, and breathe in the good.

A lot of the time, when we're going through difficulties, we might ask ourselves: 'Why is everything going wrong, and why is that happening now?' And it has a knock-on effect, so then maybe your car doesn't start or you can't find a parking space and you generally feel really down. Your guides and spirits are waiting around for you to say the word and ask them for help. If you don't ask them for help, you won't receive any because they're not allowed to interfere with the universal law. I always come back to my spirit guides for help.

As well as asking for help, you need to also look for signs. People walk around with blinkers on a lot of the time. Signs can be anything that has meaning to you and brings you comfort. This can be a written article, different trees and flowers, certain numbers, a type of animal or something in nature, like a butterfly or feather appearing from nowhere. For example, when a good friend of mine died of cancer, her funeral was on a Friday in December and the clouds were black. It was pouring with rain, but while in the church, we saw butterflies flying around. I know that was her spirit being present with us. Whenever Ingrid and I had a problem, or rather, a situation as I prefer to label it, it could be the middle of winter and freezing outside when we would see butterflies in our bedroom. It was a sign that our dear friend was sending love and helping us, so we would say 'thank you'.

A few years ago, Ingrid and I were working in America and she was giving a reading for our friend, Martin, in the healing room. I was sitting in a deck chair outside in the sunlight, enjoying the weather and doing a bit of meditating, when a big butterfly landed on my hand and stayed there for about 10 minutes. When Ingrid and Martin came out, Ingrid told me that Martin's reading was all about butterflies. It was confirmation to Martin that what she was saying about this butterfly, about the status of his life and what he should be doing, was true. I knew in my gut that this was a sign because it came to me as well. The biggest sign that people tend to get but ignore is their gut feeling. Just follow the signposts that are brought into your life, and you'll be fine.

I'm 64 now, and I've always said that when I get near my mid-60s, life is going to take off even more for me. What I want to do before I pass on and go back to spirit is set up a trust or a foundation; focus on teaching. I would like to buy this retreat that we are sitting in now for future generations to be able to come here to study and get complementary therapy, for the community to get treatment. Ideally, I'd love to be able to offer one free day a week to those who can't afford complementary therapy. I'd like to do more travelling and pass on my knowledge.

Here with Ingrid and my mum, both so supportive in my work.

Me on my 50th birthday, letting my hair down.

13

RELIGION AND SPIRITUALITY

I believe that all religions come back to love and the importance of taking care of each other. They all have the basis of doing good, but unfortunately, being humans, it hasn't worked out that way. I think religion is too controlling. I've experienced that because I belonged to the Church of England. I was a Sunday school teacher to begin with.

My second wife Sandra and I used to teach every Sunday. The kids had a great time, and Sandra was amazing at it. I was teaching for a year before becoming a church warden and going on to do an alpha course, researching different bits of Bible texts. I used to love going to church. But all the people who used to come to my church were doctors, lawyers, etc., and I started questioning what our mission was. We were taught to help the poor, but there were no poor people coming to our church. I didn't see any efforts to help people in the community who needed it. I never had a conversation with anyone about it, and I think, at that time in my life, I wasn't confident enough to raise it.

I was still going to church when I got into reiki. And when the vicar found out, he came to our house and told me I was working with the devil. He said that if I was working with evil and if I didn't stop it, then I would no longer be welcome at church. That was when I stopped going to church.

By working with energy and stepping into that new life, my confidence went sky-high. The people I had given healing treatments to all had a 100% positive effect, so it wasn't an option for me to give it up. I must have always known that there was something else out there from when I used to pray as a child. Coming from a butchery background, full of male ego and testosterone, I didn't really believe in all this spirituality and energy stuff. I had no idea just how much of an effect it would have on my life.

We should be kind to everyone, no matter who they are. None of us are entitled to make a judgement. Just try to accept and give love. Be understanding and show compassion.

Me and Silvana playing Gong on island Vis Croatia, Soul plan retreat.

Playing drum with a group on a soul plan retreat on Island Vis Croatia.

Performing Drum Journey on Island Vis.

Jenny and me with Gong Master Don Conreaux in Zagreb Croatia.

14

MY SONS

I've always felt that I owe David and Daniel something. When they were born, I worked extremely long hours, and I wasn't able to be with them as much as I would have liked. They were five and six years old when their mum, Carla, left me and took them. I would only have them every two weekends but, with no money, I was living in one room with my girlfriend's family and couldn't treat them in the way I would have liked to.

David and I get on really well. He is a year older than Daniel. We try to go away once a year together, just for a weekend. We talk about everything, so we're more like mates than father and son, but we also have that great paternal relationship. Daniel took me and Ingrid in when we first got together and had nowhere to go. We moved out of the hotel into his home, when his wife had recently given birth to their twins. We stayed with them for two weeks and a wonderful, joyous time.

Daniel has struggled. I haven't had a lot to do with Daniel

because he got into drugs and is unable to overcome his addictions. Many times in the past, I have offered for him to come to me for as long as he wanted. I wanted him to try to work with me and all the therapies that we have to get him off drugs. But that didn't work out. I think he would make a very good healer. They both would.

Letting go has been quite a hard lesson for me over the years. From the moment your child is born, your role as a parent is to teach but let go. They do not belong to you. They have their own journey, and your job is to show them how this system works on Earth and advise them along the way. I had some of that knowledge when this was happening with Daniel and, as hard as it is for parents to let go, I learned to come to terms with that. I often wonder if I have done enough for him, if I could have done more, but however painful it is, I have to accept that this is his journey.

I have found that people with very sensitive energies need an escape, and that can often be through alcohol or drugs because they can't cope with this low vibrational situation on Earth. As a family, we have tried to help him, as we all feel a responsibility towards him, but it has affected us all, so we had to back off. In that sense, Daniel has been teaching us in his own way.

David was clinging on, trying to do everything to help his brother. He was paying for Daniel to go to top rehabilitation clinics, but nothing worked. So it's really been a lesson in letting go. We mustn't hold on to the concept that family is everything and force relationships. We are all on our own journey, and family is more than just who you are blood-related to. We also have our spiritual or soul families.

The mission for each soul is to gather information from their group so they can learn. The souls coming out of that family will go into different situations. They come together to help us get through life. A soul family is just other humans who have come from your spiritual family. Ingrid and I are an example. We are twin flames, and we found each other to learn and exchange information and to create all of this.

My two sons, left to right: Daniel and David with their children, Lauren, Leah and Olivia.

Me and David at a ELO concert.

Daniel and David with Mum behind them.

15

THE KINDNESS OF OTHERS

I t is important to me that I recognise the good fortune that I have experienced in my life through the altruism of others. I also think it is an important life lesson for us all to practise giving to others with positive intent and not expecting anything in return.

There are two very special people who have made my dreams a reality, and without them I would not have achieved what I have nor would I have overcome my self-limiting beliefs.

I would like to introduce them at this point of the book because now that you understand the life that I have lived, I hope you can see how a simple gesture of goodwill can completely transform a person's destiny, and you may not even be aware that you were the one responsible for it, but that does not matter. What does matter is the chain of events that you set off in the universe, which can bring about positive change to anyone that you meet.

To the receiver, be aware of the goodwill of others and be

willing to accept it. I do not think that it was a coincidence that these two women appeared in my life to help me when they did, for I had started my journey of enlightenment and I had communicated to the universe that I was ready.

Jane Dale

I have known Jane for about 40 years. I first met her when I was the Continental meat manager for the Coop in Cambridge. Jane and her husband were responsible for conducting all the training for the various meat departments.

I remember one day, I was sitting in the staff room and observing Jane delivering a training session and I thought I would like to do that one day, and 25 years later I did!

I started off by doing all of my butchery training courses with Jane and her husband before I moved to Wales. She has always kept in contact with me, but we didn't see each other after I moved, and when I moved back to England, I was no longer able to work due to my illness, so we didn't see each other then either.

At that point we hadn't spoken for a couple of years, but still she never forgot me. It was one of those friendships where we might have had a few gaps, but we could always pick up where we left off. So when Jane called me, I was busy telling her all about my illness and moving back home, but I had no idea that her husband had died a year earlier.

That's Jane. She was asking all about how I was doing

without telling me about herself. She had been going through a terrible time but still found the time to call me and ask how I was.

When I moved back to March and went through the process of healing myself, Jane, who by now was in frequent contact with me, suggested to me that as I had so much experience because of all the various places I had worked that I should become an assessor for her.

But it meant that I had to go back to studying and sitting exams again, which I hated because it was so difficult for me.

Initially, I turned her down because of the volume of paperwork involved, but she managed to convince me, and she guided me through the whole process, and she even paid for me to get my qualifications.

I used to drive from March to Ipswich to take part in the course, and for the whole journey, I would be so absolutely terrified that I would feel physically sick at times. There was a lot of vocabulary that I had to learn and a lot of bureaucratic jargon that I had to know, so I really didn't enjoy it, but Jane continued to support and encourage me, and thanks to her I passed the course. I then started to work for her as an assessor travelling all around the country. Jane also paid for me to do an advanced management course, and I have even trained other student assessors for her as a senior assessor. I have worked in Cairo for her, and we carried out a training course in Dubai together.

I am currently working with her again, and the college

has won every award in the industry, and we have been classed as the best training provider in the country for what we do, but amazingly, it still has a small, family-run business feel to it, and Jane still has full control.

Jane wanted to make a complete success of the college on behalf of her late husband, which is a wonderful tribute to him.

Everything that I learned by going through that process of studying and then becoming an assessor has helped me with all of my complementary therapy work as I once again became a student and then the teacher.

I never could have thought that my career as a butcher would blend into my life as a complementary therapist, and that has been a valuable lesson for me to experience that everything happens for a reason and at the right time.

Lynn O'Sullivan

After I completed my reiki training, I felt I needed to learn more skills, and I was interested in reflexology. I asked one of my reiki contacts who told me she knew of the perfect teacher; her name was Lynn, and she was fantastic and taught at an adult education college in Stansted.

I remember the day I called her. It was a Monday morning, and I was sitting on the floor looking out of my patio window while on the phone to Lynn, and she told me she had a clinical reflexology course starting in two weeks that I could enrol onto.

Once again, I felt out of my depth. Bear in mind that I had no college qualifications, I could hardly read and had minimal computer skills and that this educational course was the first one I had done since leaving school at 14 and it was nearly to degree level.

On the Monday morning that the course began, I was driving to Stansted, and I was absolutely terrified at the thought of taking on such an intense level of learning. During this time, I was also still out of work, so money was an issue, but I had managed to get help through an organisation that helps people with disabilities to get back into work by helping financially with vocational courses.

Generally in a reflexology class, there will be about 10– 15 women and rarely any men; however on that morning, there were two other men besides myself: another Steven, who was a carpenter and who was also dyslexic like me and very nervous, and John, who was a bricklayer, so the three of us instantly gravitated towards each other and were very close throughout the course.

I used to stay up most of the night to complete my studies. I would type everything up on my computer because it had spell check and I was so slow because I could only type with one finger at a time, but I persevered throughout the year-long course, and I passed every level.

From that moment on, Lynn hasn't been able to get rid of me! I went on to complete a handful of various courses with her such as Swedish body massage, Sports massage, Indian head massage, and aromatherapy.

While I was completing these courses, Lynn and I developed a real connection, and six months after I had finished the courses, I was teaching taster sessions for reflexology in the classroom next to her thanks to her belief in me, and those students would go on to enrol in the full course with Lynn, so we were a great team.

At the time when Lynn started teaching at the college, I think there were only about 10 people who enrolled each year, and by the time she left, there were about 400 a year. Unfortunately, she was made redundant due to government funding cuts.

We have become lifelong friends. Ingrid and I used to take Lynn and her husband to Belgium, and we had various weekends away with them as well.

She also used to let Ingrid and me teach reiki in her house on many weekends and would recommend people to join my course and make herself scarce so we could have the whole house uninterrupted, which was incredibly kind of her.

Sadly, her husband passed away three years ago, and I am going with her to The Maldives in September to scatter his ashes, and I will perform a ceremony in his honour as well.

If it wasn't for Lynn, I don't think I would have learned all of the extra complementary therapies, which all led me to opening my retreat. My wish is for Lynn to join me here at the Terra Nova School of Light and teach courses again as she has gone into helping people as a counsellor but teaching complementary therapy is her passion, and it would be a wonderful way to thank her if I could bring her back to do what she loves doing.

Me and my cousin doing a sales promotion in my shop for J.H. Dewhurst in Harrow. Good times.

Me teaching Butchery in Egypt Cairo for meat Ipswich.

Me teaching Reiki to my teacher of complementary Therapies, Lynne.

Me with Jane, on my left, and all the guys from Eat Ipswich on our award night out.

16

LOVE, FORGIVENESS, AND THE UNIVERSE

I want people to really believe and realise that they are so much more than they think they are. We are in this human body and we have limitations, but that's so that we can learn lessons through perseverance. Try to break out of the limitations you have put upon yourself, and don't deny yourself the endless possibilities that life has to offer.

I was told that I wasn't smart enough to achieve anything, so I shouldn't bother trying. But at the age of 60, I started having flying lessons. I never would have been able to learn to fly if I hadn't embraced a pure determination to just try. I passed three out of my nine exams with 100%, and the others I passed at 85–90%.

Don't give up. Always believe that things are possible. Don't let money rule you. People have so much fear around money. I have done all the things I have wanted to do and I didn't have the money, but somehow things always worked out. I've had a full life. I've been all over the world and done so many different things.

People think that if they just ask, it should just happen, and then stop believing because it doesn't happen. You've got to do the work. You've got to do tests and overcome the challenges and show your faith.

I want to thank everyone who will read this. I hope you will feel the energy and the love coming out of this book. Hopefully, it will plant seeds, give you motivation and energise you.

My spirit drum that I use for Healings.

The first two Gongs that I brought.

Me preparing the plane before a flying lesson.

Me with Kevin Keegan on our award night out with Meat Ipswich.

StoryTerrace

Printed in Great Britain
by Amazon

11493071R00084